In

My

Own

Words

(Poetry of Life)

BY: LONNIESHA JACKSON

MANUFACTURED BY

TPL Publications LLC

CONTACT INFORMATION

WEBISTE:
http://tplpublications.com

EMAIL:
thepoeticlounge@gmail.com

ADDRESS:

CEO/Fiordaliza Charles
7014 13TH AVE SUITE 202
BROOKLYN NY 11228-1604

INTRODUCTION

Poetry could be described in various ways; in my personal opinion, I find that poetry is the window to one's heart. I also believe that poetry is not as appreciated as it should be.

Poetry is the true expressions of a poet, usually expressed in a matter that may shock the audience so that, they want more of it. A poet often uses poetry to showcase his or her true emotions freely.

Poetry could also be used as a positive reinforcement if used correctly; it could help to heal an injured heart. I also found that there is no right or wrong way to write poetry, no matter how the poet uses his or her words; they can add and take out emotions each and every time.

When it comes to my poetry I just express my heart, I hope that "In my own words" will reach your hearts because I created each poem with you in mind. Thank you for your support & Feedback.

Lonniesha "FloetPoet" Jackson

ACKNOWLEDGMENTS

Thank you God, without you I am nothing.

***

Thank you mama, for your unconditional love and support

***

Thanks to the people at TPL that worked so hard to make assure that this book was completed.

Special Thanks to the CEO Fiordaliza Charles for welcoming me with open arms, To Publisher/Editor Ms. Staxx Cordero for taking the time to enhance my book and to Book Designer; Mr. Duane Crockett for the wonderful job he did on my book cover.

***

Last but not least thanks to all my readers because of your support, I have more reasons to write

DEDICATION

Poetry be still in my heart; make my emotions come alive and perhaps touch my readers, what an amazing feeling. I adore Poetry and it chose me at a very young age. For, this is my gift to you in my own words.

Dedicated to the Poet in you.

"FloetPoet"

TABLE OF CONTENTS

FORGIVENESS

1

One of the most courageous things

Is having the power

To forgive

To forget

To have control

When you feel like all is lost

When you just want to give it all up

To open your heart

and know that you are doing

A wonderful thing

Knowing that you can whole heartedly

Forgive and forget

To realize

Life is too short, to hold grudges

Unable to ever let go

Living with that, can be the worst feeling

One can incur

The power of the mind, the body & the soul

To love, to live, to learn

New things everyday

Blissful blessings abundantly upon thee

The power of forgiving

THE POWER OF ONE'S HEART

2

When you love anyone

You should

Get the full love in return

If not

Maybe it's not really love

To be unable to love

To be loved back

To never experience

Such a great adventure

as love

To not know the feeling

of real life butterflies

Inside ones stomach

That tingling sensation

When he or she enters a room

To know

When the one, looks into your eyes

You truly

Are the one person

They really do see

You make their heart smile

To forever be

INDEED LOVE IS IN

3

When you look into my eyes

There's no surprise

To what you are thinking

When you lick your lips

Give me, that gorgeous smile

I become warm and tingly all over

I giggle like a school girl

Blush & smile

You caress my face

Run your fingers through

my hair

Whew baby! Love is in the air

Gazing deeply into each other's eyes

I can't imagine

Being without you

My one

My only

My love, my pain, my rock,

My heart and my soul

My man, my friend

There is no end

To the love, that I carry for you

My soul brother

This love here is for you and no other

THESE WORDS TO YOU

4

I see you

Watching me

All of the time

I pass it off

And walk on by

You think you are slick

You think you are real cool

Looking at me

You must think you see a fool

Cool, you think you know so much

Little do you know?

I wrote the book on running games

Dropping them lines

At the snap of my fingers

At the twist of my hips

The flash of my smile

I could have you, under my spell

Your ears open to the words

Only I can tell

My soft sensual touch

Would be all your tired body needs

So relax and just chill

You will be just fine

Make yourself comfortable

While I get the wine

TAKE A WALK WITH ME

5

Take my hand and take a walk with me

To a place where we can just be

Whatever we want

For as long as we need

Just you

Just me

The moments that are shared with you

Are deeply cherished

Forever within me

I can honestly say that I will love you forever

This I know

Because when someone makes your soul

SMILE.......Then

That's a rare love

Take a walk with me

Far and wide

I love being your woman

Always by your side

Take a walk with me

Down that aisle

Where forever is ours

CONSTANTLY AVOIDING

6

Wherever you are

I don't want to be

You are coming my way

I completely turn around

I will never speak to you again

No matter what comes out of your mouth

I just can't stand you anymore

Call me mean

Call me selfish

I just do not care

As long as you aren't actually calling me

Let's be honest, fair is fair

Please go on about your way

There is no turning back

What's done is done

I am determined to move on

That I must do

To never have to see your face

Again is such a relief

All the letters

Return to sender

All the flowers, out the door

Nothing else to do with you

Please stop sending gifts

I can't take it anymore

WHEN LOVE ISN'T ENOUGH

7

We have tried to make it work

Lately, trying to make it work

Doesn't even work

It's like we are strangers

In our own home

We don't even sleep together

Sometimes

You don't even come home

You say, it's just work

Trying to get caught back up

But through your words

All I hear are lies

We've always said that we would

Never lie to each other

I just don't know

What to do anymore. Should I leave?

Or stay and tough it out

I've done my part

You are the one with all the lies

Nightly excuses

I am tired of nightly cries

I love you so much

I don't think you ever knew

When love isn't enough...What do you do?

SEARCHING FOR THE ONE

8

Too short

Too cocky

A real pretty boy

Another one he looks like

He may be a jockey

Doesn't speak English well

No job

No car

No goals

What in the world?

I've searched high

I've searched low

I've been searching so long

That I should be getting paid

Looking for a man

Is no easy task

But could I just find

A nice looking man

With a job and a car

Who knows how to treat a woman?

Likes to go out from time to time

Makes me laugh until I cry

Is it too much to ask

AFTER ALL THIS TIME

9

I haven't seen him in years

Until

One day I saw him at the gas station

I kept on my way

Until

I heard my name

Called from his mouth

I stopped in my tracks

Collected myself & turned around

Hello, I said

My mind went completely blank

from there

So I decided to turn back around

Simply just walked away

Wait a minute, he said

He finished pumping his gas

I took a few deep breaths

Then he was there

Right there, in my face

You look good, so do you

We, were so nervous

Clearly

It was in the air

Are you seeing anyone?

No

Good, neither am I

Let's have dinner tonight

We have a lot of catching up to do

By the way, I've missed you

Yeah, I missed you too and after

All this time

REMEMBER US

10

Do you ever just remember us?

When we first met

When we went on our first date

When we first kissed

When we first made love

Do you ever just remember us?

Our first fight

Our first make-up

Our daily routines

Our first child

Do you ever just remember us?

Our wedding day

Our first house

Our first dog

Do you ever just remember us?

Like I do

Like I wish we could go back to

The days when we still loved one another

We, would do anything to protect each other

I would do anything to get it all back

But I can't

So, all I can do is

Just remember us

LITTLE GIRL LOST WRITING FOUND

11

Growing up on the streets

Wasn't something a young child

should have to do

A girl non the less

But when you don't know

Who your father is and your mother

Out there in the world

In love with that pipe

The drugs and the pain

The last time I saw her

She didn't even know my name

I was on my own

I was determined to make it

Never gave up

Never knew how

I started learning things

about myself

I had to learn, how to lie

Lie like I never thought

I would ever have to do

How else could I explain?

How was it possible?

For me to be in school all day

Homeless at night

I was just a child

Where were my parents?

Who got me ready for school each day?

I blended in like the other kids

The lost soul of a child

I started writing in between

Homework and finding my next meal

Finding somewhere; safe and clean to sleep

I wrote about everything

Anything

I wrote real life

I wrote about struggles

I wrote short stories

I graduated from high school

Into College but

The thing I'm most proud of

I wrote myself off of the streets

Into my first home

I wrote a name for myself

I wrote to save my life

I was once a little girl lost

My writing found

FACING OBSTACLES

12

Anytime you break up with someone

You are going to experience various emotions

Maybe you have never felt like this before

You never know

How something really is

Until

You are the one going through it

There may be tears

Always some fears

but you survive

You get strong

Stronger by the day

Determined to let nothing

get in your way

Of being happy

Reaching goals

and fulfilling dreams

No matter what life

throws at you

Dodge it and

keep it moving

HOT NIGHT

13

When you caress my body

With your strong masculine hands

This feeling comes over me

That, I cannot explain

I'm aroused

in ways that only

You

Can make occur

Your kisses

On the back of my neck

While you are pulling my hair

The smell of hot sweet love

Floats thickly in the air

We're both sweating beyond belief

My body drips for you

Soaking wet

Love between us, intense

Our chemistry

Has always been cosmic

Amazing to no end

Your lips feel so good

All over my body

May this night never end

Morning comes as we lay

A SUMMER DAY

14

As I walked along the beach

The beautiful spotlight sun above me

The warm sand between my toes

There was such a cool breeze

The weather was perfect for a swim

Perfect to fish

Perfect to feel

Perfect to get lost in the sand

To be found in the deep blue

Like a bird on the back of a whale

Sitting so perfectly while floating

Not a care in the world

Glistening beneath the sun

I LOVE YOU

15

When I am with you

It feels like

we're the only two in the world

It's like

I am on a cloud that never came down

You truly make me so happy

You give my butterflies, butterflies

I still get nervous and shy

I love you so much

That it feels unreal

Hard to believe, I can love someone so much

And for him to actually love me back

He treats me like a queen

To have someone

That, will do anything in the world

For me

When I feel lost and alone

I know I can always count on him

We are more than lovers

We started off as good friends

Now

He is my husband

I've never been so happy

In my life

Until

The day, I became his wife

It's nothing but joy ever since

DESPERATELY LONGING YOU

16

Desperate to feel your touch

Longing to smell your cologne

Restless because I can no longer sleep

Pain because I feel my heart breaking

Disbelief that you are gone

Alone, that's how you left me

In denial to the fact

We may never get back together again

Surviving the constant reminders of you

Of us

Desperate to feel whole again

Longing to see your face

Wishing to get another chance

Hoping, you'd walk through the door

If you never come back

One thing I can keep

The love I had for you

All the memories

Good and bad

But that terrible fight

I wish we never had

I cannot go back into time

I can't change a thing

I can only move ahead towards

the future

And finally let go of the past

MISSING

17

Alone, dark and so cold

Can anybody hear me?

There is no sound

I hear no cars

I hear no trains

Even no sound of airplanes

No dogs

No cats

Alone in a small room

Dark as can be

Handcuffed around my wrists

With shackles on my feet

Is anyone even looking for me?

Does anyone know I'm gone?

I can't believe this has happened

No one saw anything

No one heard a sound

MAKE LOVE TO ME

18

Make love to me

Make me feel

Like a woman should

Caress my face

Run your fingers through my hair

Tell me, that I am beautiful

Make love to me

Make my body completely melt

I am all yours

Dominate me

Dominate my love

Make love to me

Make me lose all control

From head to toe

Mind, body and soul

I will be whatever you want

Whomever you want

Make love to me

Let me fulfill all your fantasies

I will make your dreams come true

Make love to me

Make me cry

Make me feel you

Let me feel you

Feel me

Feel each other

Make love to me and let me never

Know the pain of being alone

DARK AREAS OF US

19

I never thought

We would have so many problems

In our relationship

I never thought the day would come

When we could not talk

A dark cloud

Has been over us a while now

I never thought that

You would ever

physically harm me

You did though

Many, many, times

I was terrified to leave

Terrified to say a word

You always said you never meant it

Like a fool, I believed you

You broke my arm, split my lip

Blackened both eyes

Sent me to the hospital

for three weeks one time

Again, you apologized

Again, I was your fool

It was never that severe again

But your abuse

Seemed to have no end

I just don't know how

You love someone

Why hurt them repeatedly

You should never

had wanted to see me that way

I finally got a backbone

I found the strength to leave you

It was so hard

It had to be done though

You definitely need help

You have a serious problem

You really thought it was okay

You were wrong

I'm glad I am gone

Compared, to what I went through with you

I am better off alone

THE WAY I FEEL FOR YOU

20

The way I feel for you

I can honestly say

I have never felt this way

About any other man

The way I feel for you

It sometimes

Completely stops me

In my tracks

I can't think at times

My vision blurred

I get so nervous

Anxious beyond belief

I can't wait to see your face

To hear your voice

To smell your sexy cologne

To feel your soft juicy lips

To feel your big strong hands

All over my body

The way I feel for you

Its love

It's real

It is real love

The way I feel for you

I loved you then

Now and forever

TELL ME WHY?

21

Tell me why?

You walked away

Deciding to give up

after all this time

Tell me why?

You broke my heart

Tell me why?

You act as if you do not care

I just don't know where we went wrong

I cannot believe all of this

has happened

Tell me why?

Why don't you love me anymore?

Tell me why?

You don't want me

As much as I still want you

I feel so lost

Helpless, like a child

There is nothing I can do

I am no longer in control

Tell me why?

It was so easy for you

Show me how?

You feel no pain

To look at my face

Not feeling a thing

Tell me why?

I am the only one

Heartbroken

To never see your face again

To never hear your mouth

utter my name

To never feel

Your hands

Against my skin, again

Tell me why?

It hurts so badly

FOREVER YOURS

22

Even though

We are not together anymore

I still can't help thinking of you

Every once in a while

I often wonder

What might have been?

If we hadn't had that awful fight

If we did get married

Instead of walking away

If, I could do it all over again

Things would be done differently

I could never see myself without you

Somehow, I have made it through

It's been hard but possible

I must move on

All the pain,

the hate and so many tears

We both have made decisions

That, we must live with

To know

That, it is truly over

No more we

No more us

To know

You truly hurt me deeply

I can't explain

That is forever yours

LOVE IS

23

When a love is lost

Sometimes, it is never found

You cannot force it back

It must follow on its own

It is basically out of your control

No matter how you feel

No matter what you have done

It's even possible

The one you love

May not be the one

Your mind tells you things

That your heart does not know

The heart feels deeper

than the mind allows

Love is special

Love is life

To love is lovely

Love is love

Indeed a beautiful thing

FEAR RAISES ITS UGLY HEAD

24

Don't know what to say

You left me speechless

When you uttered those four words

Will You Marry Me?

You really sent a shock to the system

As much as I would love to say yes

I just can't right now

I feel as if we are not ready

Marriage is a lot of responsibility

Marriage is teamwork

Marriage is a job

Marriage is supposed to be forever

The bond between a husband and wife

Use to be unbreakable

Society doesn't honor

The sacred vows

Of marriage anymore

The cheating and lies

The sad alibis

The hurt

The destruction of family

The pain of the truth

The pain from the pain

I guess you can say

I am afraid

I don't want

Our marriage to crumble

I want us to be perfect

But I know

There is no such thing

I don't want to be another statistic

Within the married world

I don't want to lose you either

I am beside myself with fear

FINALLY SAYING GOODBYE

25

I drove you to the airport

You don't know how hard that was for me

Knowing, that you weren't coming back

It kills me inside

To know

We will never see each other again

We loved each other

as much as two people could

We said, we would remain friends

Honestly, can I be your friend?

You

The man

Which I was always

in love with

The man

That, was always by my side

The man

I would do anything for

Me

The woman

You loved

with all your heart

Why were we finally saying goodbye

Something, I thought we would never do

WHEN THINGS CHANGE

26

I sold the house

Moved out of town

Just couldn't stand it anymore

With you not around

I am starting over again

New city, new house, new job

New beginnings

I am doing the best I can

To survive

To maintain

To stay strong

To never give up

You know me better than that

Inside I am dying

To go back home

To be with you again, to our life

Our house, our city

Now, it's like we never existed

Funny how soon we forget

When things change

THESE KIND WORDS

27

Say, you love me

Let me, hear your love

Show me, you love me

Let me, feel your love

Your words are so strong

I can see them

Coming out of your mouth

Knowing, that you love me

Gives me strength to carry on

Your love, is like my drug

I am so addicted

You quench my thirst

You fill my hunger

I look into your eyes

I see me

I see you

I see you and me

I see us

I see you

Looking back

at me with love

You have such a big heart

Kind, caring a very good man

Would be so lost without you

Could not stand to be alone

Just knowing

I am in your thoughts

Keeps you near

ONCE UPON A TIME

28

Once upon a time

We were young

We were cool

Once upon a time

You loved me

And I loved you

Once upon a time

we were married

We had babies

We were engaged

Once upon a time

We truly, were in love

Once upon a time

You were my man

And I was your girl

Once upon a time

We were strangers

Once upon a time

You walked up to me

and said hi

I said hello

Once upon a time

We went on our first date

Once upon a time

Such a long time ago

KNOCKING AT MY DOOR

29

I hung up the phone

Shutting the chapters of our book

This has been going on

for years now

When will we learn?

Now

You are knocking at my door

Should I answer?

or let you stand out in the cold

I just don't know what to do

I thought things

would be simpler now

Instead, you are knocking at my door

To let you in means

Letting you back in

In my home

In my heart

In my life

Not sure if I am ready

For any of that again

So, continue knocking at my door

SITTING HERE LISTENING

30

Once again

You're just going on & on

While I am sitting here listening

Wondering...why?

I have been with you for so long

You are never satisfied, always complaining

Every other word out your mouth is
negative

Sitting here, I am listening to you

I just cannot take it anymore

If you say one more word

I will scream

While, pulling my hair from the roots

Sitting here, listening to you

LET'S NOT PRETEND

31

Let's not pretend

That you didn't want us to end

I'm not playing

These childish games with you

If you want me good

If not then let me go

Playing with my heart

Is what you're not going to do

Let's not pretend

As if you

Had everything under control

Just be a man

Own up, to your many mistakes

You are weak instead

Let's not pretend

We, both decided

To take time apart

It was the best decision

We've made in a long time

So please, let's not pretend

LOVING MYSELF NOW

32

I can't imagine

What's going on in your head now?

What I do know is

I am taking some me time

It's well over due

But better late than never

I am going to buy

Myself something nice

First, I'm going to start

Loving myself

Now

Obviously

I didn't while we were together

If I did

I wouldn't have allowed you to treat

Me the way you did

I often wondered

Did you even love me?

Who really knows?

It doesn't even matter now

I'm living life and loving it

Loving myself having fun

Going to find a man

Who makes me his number one

I guess, I should say thanks

For opening up my eyes

To see

That you are not

Who I should be with

Now

I am loving myself

SOMETHING TO SAY

33

I have something to say

Not sure

If you are going to like it

I have something to say

You may be mad

You may be hurt

You may be confused

You may

Even have something to say

Fighting, with myself

To get my words out right

I have something to say

I am afraid

I am anxious

I am confused

I do not know

Can I go through with this?

I have something to say

But

I don't know how to say it

YOUR WAY OR NOTHING ELSE

34

So demanding and controlling

As if, you are someone's boss

We supposed to be a team

Partners,' a united front

When something goes wrong

It's always

Your way or nothing else

That's not fair at all

Your way or nothing else

Is what

I am constantly hearing

Why are you like this?

Who do you think you are?

I can't take it anymore

You are driving me crazy

To the point, that I don't want

to be with you anymore

Yes, I love you

But

That's really not enough

To keep me here

I really never imagined

that we would end like this

You made it this way

With all of your strict rules

I cannot, will not

follow them anymore

So now

You go your way

I'm going mine

and

There's nothing else to say

WRITING MY HEART TO YOU

35

I am writing you this letter

Maybe

it can help you understand

Why?

I love you so much

Why?

You are a special man

I am writing my heart to you

So, you can feel my love

Read my words

So, they will touch your heart and soul

I want you to sincerely feel

How I feel for you

I love you

I love loving you

I want you

I need you

Maybe, these words will touch you

So, that you will finally know

I am writing my heart to you

If you need to

Write to me too

I will explore your words

With, my mind and heart

I will feel your love for me

Writing, your heart to me

COMPARING US TO WHAT

36

Thinking back

On our relationship

I definitely would say

We were never perfect

Far from it

As of matter of fact

When you love someone

You do all you can

Trying,

with all your might

Never giving up

But now though

Comparing us to what

When we always fight

Can't agree on anything

Never seeing eye to eye

Comparing us to what?

When we are constantly

Screaming, at each other

No longer, sleeping in the same bed

Comparing us to what?

When we no longer eat dinner together

Living in two different areas of the house

Comparing us to what?

When we, have completely fallen apart

No amount of glue could put our

Broken pieces back together

Compared to what?

When there is nothing left

BEING A WOMAN

37

I wake up every morning

Take a look in the mirror

I see a woman

I am a woman

I love being a woman

Being a woman

Means

To experience

Once in a lifetime changes

To begin, your menstrual cycle

To experience, your first kiss

Your first love

To be asked to the prom

Being a woman

Doesn't mean you are helpless

You don't always need a man

To help you with certain things

Being a woman

Means

You can do just as much

As any man does

Being a woman

Is a wonderful thing

Being a woman

Means to carry a child

Give birth to a child

Some of the greatest pleasures as

To being a woman

BEFORE & AFTER

38

Before we met

I never knew how

Deep love could really go

After we met

Things I discovered

That I

never thought I'd know

Before I said

I love you

We still showed

that we genuinely

Cared for one another

After, we both said it

We knew it was true

Before we lived together

We often talked about it

Wondering

How would it be?

After

we moved in together

Then we knew

We were, doing the right thing

Before we had children

We talked about everything

What type of parents

We thought we'd be

After, we had children

They were

all we talked about

Nothing more we enjoyed

than being parents

Before, we got married

There were so many things

that needed to be done

After, we got married

We knew

it was the best decision

MY DEEPEST DESRIRE

39

To have you alone

No more playing games

Having the confidence

To say

How I feel about you

My deepest desire

If I, could only make you see

That regardless

of what may happen

You are the man for me

My deepest desire

The passion inside of me

For you

The passion inside of you

For me

My deepest desire

No one

Knows me like you do

You are the only man

I let my guard down with

With you

I am never shy

With you

I am never nervous

With you

I can be myself

My deepest desire

I carry you in my soul

You are

My deepest desire

THINK AGAIN

40

If you think

You've got the best of me

Think again

Luckily

I have always landed on my feet

When it comes to you

Your sticky situations

If you think

You are going to make me feel bad

About myself

Think again

I am beautiful

Strong and capable

of being on my own

If you think

I'm going to cry myself to sleep at nights

Those days

are long gone now

I won't do you the favor

of letting a tear fall

If you think

I am going to beg you

to work it out

Think again

Breaking up

Was the best thing

For us to do

If you think

I am going to miss you

Yes, I will, that is true

But you

Better think again if you think

I will ever get back with you

LETS' TALK ABOUT IT

41

Lets' talk about it

To see

What's on each other's mind?

Hoping

We're on the same page

Maybe, we can come up with

some type of compromise

Lets' talk about it

and see

How well we

actually do know one another

Lets' talk about it

To define

What our relationship

is really about

Lets' talk about it

To find out

if we need to be talking

Or

Walking away never looking back

THE MAN NEXT DOOR

42

The man next door

Moved in about three weeks ago

He appears to live alone

He is very quiet

The man next door

A very handsome man

I must admit

Very nice body as well

Couldn't help but notice

while he

Was mowing the lawn one day

The man next door

Has a beautiful smile

It definitely brightens my day

I sometimes

carry small conversations

With the man next door

He tells me I look nice

Says

He likes my new hairdos

Me and the man next door

Have been spending

a lot of time together, lately

I enjoy our time together

How do I tell?

The man next door

That

I love him

And he has my heart

NO LONGER HAPPY

43

It seems like all we do is argue

It's so hard to get a long now

As much as I love you

As much as I want

things to be right, again

I don't think it can

No longer happy

with you

No longer happy

with me

Or us

I know you feel the same way

If neither of us are happy anymore

Why?

Try to salvage something

Maybe isn't worth saving at all

I feel so bad, saying these things

Without speaking to you

To know, how you feel

What do you want?

So many emotions

My mind can't contain

I really don't know

what to do

What do I need to do?

What needs to be done?

I do know

I am no longer happy

PASSIONATE

44

I am passionate about you

I am passionate about us

I am passionate

About the love we share

We are passionate lovers

It's deep

It's real

It's good, so good

It's overwhelmingly breath taking

To be so passionately in love

With a man

Who is passionately in love?

With me

Our passion is passionate

That is a love so deep

To crave one another

To even feel their presence

When they're not around

To yearn

For that one body

For the heart beats as one

APPRECIATING THE UNAPPRECIATIVE

45

I appreciate

The many things

You have taught me

You have always

been a good person

I have always told you

Aside that

I never understood

How?

You can be

so dissatisfied all of the time

Whatever is done is never enough

Whatever is said is negative

Sometimes rough

Things like that

make me stronger

More than you

could ever believe

I can't believe

How you never appreciate anything

Worse than that

I love you very much

I become weak

When you're not around

It's been troubles

in our relationship

That, I cannot lie

By no means

Is this easy for me to say

Regardless of what

I was always appreciative

Of the unappreciative you

ALL I ASK OF YOU

46

Forgive me please

I dearly beg of you

Nothing said or done

Before this moment

Doesn't even matter

The fact that I was wrong

I was initially caught

Open your heart, to my remorse

Show me how to forgive

Don't show me away

from your love

A love that I need

That I desire

I will do whatever it takes

Whatever you want

I will do whatever you need

To get you back

Whatever it is

To make you happy again

Even if it means

Putting us to an end

I AM

47

I am black
I am proud
I am a woman
I am a proud
Black woman
I am sexy
I am smart
I am funny
I am emotional
I am understanding
I am loyal
I am a good friend
I am a lover of Poetry
I am a writer
I am a Virgo
I am ME

<u>WHAT LOVE IS CAPABLE OF</u>

48

Love shouldn't hurt

But it does

Love shouldn't weaken you

That's not always true

Love shouldn't be so hard

At times it is though

Love shouldn't make you feel

So miserable

When things aren't going so well

But again it does

Again and again

Love takes you through all

Of your emotions

Love makes you happy

Love makes you sad

When situations are bad

Love can make you mad

Love takes you up and

brings you down

Sometimes you can feel like your feet

Never touched the ground

Love makes you high

Love can make you feel so low

Love is hot

Sometimes cold

But to truly know love

That's gold

INTERRACIAL LOVE

49

You're tall

I'm short

You're skinny

I'm fat

You're white

I'm black

We get looks

For many reasons

Love comes in all shapes

In all sizes

Love sees no color

We don't care what

Anyone say

I love you...my white man

You love me...your black woman

All that matters

Black on the outside...me

White on the outside...you

Same red blood

Pumping through our veins

Same tears when sad

Same pain when hurt

Same anger when mad

What is the big deal?

What we have is so real

The only thing that matters

How we feel

SLEEPING WITH THE OTHER MAN

50

I'm having an affair

No, I'm not ashamed

I have a story to tell

When I met this man

I was going through hell

With my husband

I met a man

He was charming

He was nice

He was very attractive

I was lonely

I was lost

I was vulnerable

I lost my head

I found lust

I couldn't fight temptation

This man made me feel.

I was numb to my husband

Love was lost

Sleeping with the other man

Made me alive

Sleeping with this man

made me open

He opened my heart

He opened my eyes

He opened me

He gave me things

Things I wanted

Things I needed

Things I yearned for

Things my husband was

capable of doing

But he decided not to

That's why I don't feel bad

My husband made me last

To everything in his life

When I was his wife

The other man

made me number one

I never had to ask twice

ALL I WANT

51

All I need is you

To have me always

To take of me

All I need is you

To see me

Like I am

Like I see you

For who you are

All I need

Special moments of us

Forever in my heart

All I need is your love

All I need is your smile

All I need are your kisses

All I need

Your soft touch

I miss

All I need is for you

To read this and know

All I need is you

LEAVING HOME

52

I have lived here all my life

Never knew anything else

My family is here

The man I love is here

My friends are here

My job is here

Home, full of so many memories

Good ones

Bad ones

I went to school here

I graduated from here

Fell in love, here

After it all is said & done

It's time to move on

To bigger & better things

A whole new world

Outside of my little town

Look out, here I come

LOVE STORY

53

We met such a long time ago

Seemed to never

keep in touch very well

When I first saw him

He was the finest man

I had ever seen

So nice

So polite

Very funny

We instantly were attracted

To each other

I knew I wanted him

To be my man

I was young

So pure

Never been touched

My heart knew he

was the one I needed

To take my innocence

Instead, we lost touch

Never saw him

or spoke to him again

Until the day

He walked back into my life

We were so happy

To see one another

You could clearly see

Amazing how these things happen

I've always thought of him

From time to time

Who am I fooling?

He was always on my mind

Now it's different

We're finally together

We're older now though

He is still the finest man

I'd ever seen

I love him very much

This I hope, he always knows

As we explore our love

Further, the heart grows

CAN I SHOW YOU SOMETHING

54

Can I show you something?

Look into my eyes

Tell me what you see

When I look into your eyes

I can see more than me

Can I show you something?

Take my hand

Let me lead your way

Into my heart

Into my soul

Where your love lives

Can I show something?

Close your eyes with me

Think about when we first met

Kiss me, to feel me

My words to you

My love for you

Can I show you something?

How much I love you

SO GRATEFUL

55

Thank you, for loving me

I really know you care

Thank you, for seeing me

Always being there

Thank you, for knowing me

Better than I know myself

Thank you, for always supporting me

Closely by my side

Thank you, for teaching me

The many values of life

Showing me, it's okay

To be happy

To be free

To be positive

Always, with an open mind

Thank you, for allowing my growth

From your knowledge

With valued time

FACING THE TRUTH

56

I have evaluated the situation in my
head

Over & over and over again

I just can't understand

What really happened to us?

I thought we were happy

I thought we loved each other

I thought we were on our way

Down the aisle

I thought we were in love

Why is this happening to us?

I can't believe we can't work it out

We've always gotten past things

before

Why not now?

What's so different?

I just don't get it

You have moved out

Honestly, it doesn't get any worse

I miss you so bad

Maybe, its time I faced the truth

You're not coming back

NOTING MAKES SENSE ANYMORE

57

I adored you

You adored me

We had been together for so long

Ever since high school

You were the only man

I had ever been with

That was love

It was real and true

I was loyal, faithful devoted to

Only you

We made plans together

Things we were actually going to do

Somewhere down the line

The plans changed

I was no longer part of the decision

You left me behind

Saying I was holding you back

After all this time

Now, I'm holding you back

When I am carrying your child

MISERY IN MY SOUL

58

We're in the same home

But yet we're separated

No words

No sounds

No touch

I miss you so bad

And you're right here

Just in the next room

I am so miserable

I long to talk to you

To hear you

To feel you

For you to hear me

Desperate, for you to feel me again

The pain in my heart

Is unbearable

I want this nightmare to end

Why can't you feel my pain?

Like I feel yours

I know you're hurting

I am responsible for your pain

Let me release you of the pain in your heart

Let me release myself

Of what I've done to you

IF I COULD TAKE IT BACK

59

Those words I said to you

the other night

They hurt you bad

They hurt you deep

I saw the pain in your eyes

If I could take it back

I would

Unfortunately, I cannot

It's been killing me

To see you this way

I feel so bad about

What I've done to you

I love you with every breath

in my body

To see you unhappy

Makes me sick to my soul

If I could take that night back

It would've went any other way

But still I cannot

No matter what's said or done

You were still hurt by me

I can't stand the fact

That this has happened

And I am guilty

WHEN I GROW UP

60

When I grow up

I want to be famous

I want to be different

From anybody else

I want to have a big house

When I grow up

I want to be a doctor

Or a teacher

Or a writer

When I grow up

I can be anything I want

When I grow up

I want to be a good mother

Like mine

When I grow up

No one can tell me what to do

DEPRESSION

61

It comes without any warning

It hits you

Like a ton of bricks

The most miserable emotions

An individual can experience

The crying

The loneliness

The emptiness

The darkness

I can't eat

Or I can't stop eating

All I want to do is sleep

And that's what I usually do

I feel so alone

Helpless as can be

The constant demons I fight

Inside of me

I just don't know what to do

Can anyone please help me?

My state of mind

Lost, abused &confused

I hate that I can't help myself

At all

I try so hard

I fail then fall harder

Depression out of control

It took me completely...whole

TAINTED LOVE OF MINE

62

A situation occurred

rather unexpectedly

All parties involved

Knew the game

Deceit, betrayal, infidelity and lies

We always knew the outcome

My heart began speaking loudly

Reality faded away

I was in love

In love with a man

Another woman's man

Not just any man

My sisters' husband

And he loved me too

As much as I loved him

I wanted to be with him

I wanted him to be my husband

For, me to be his wife

Never told a soul

Put my feelings aside

Never looking back

Breaking my sister's heart

Crumbling her soul

I couldn't do

63

Decisions, decisions, decisions

What to do

What needs to be done?

How to do it

How it needs to be done

When does it need to happen?

Who is to do it

Who can do it right

It's a time & place for everything

A time for love

A time for pain

A time for hate

A strong emotion

It does exist

A time for you

A time for me

Time for everyone

To see

To see love

To see life

To feel and give

As much as you can

To hope

To dream

To become

RAVISHING LOVE

64

Tear my clothes off

Let me give myself to you

Like I've never

given to another

Let me feel your hands

All over my body

Let me feel your lips

Softly, against mine

Take me in your arms

Hold me closely

Never letting go

Let's experiment with our love

In unimaginable ways

Beautiful love will be made

Take me

I am yours to have

Any way you want

For however long

My body is yours

Like unknown territory

Discover me

Explore me

Become one inside

Thrust me deeply

With your manhood

Make me feel good

For only you know how

Make me weak

With pain

That hurts so good

Inside, I'm driven insane

An unbelievable high

Oh my...

COMPANION

65

Someone to talk to when I need it

Someone to listen

Instead of just hearing me

Someone to massage my back

Rub my feet

After a long day

Let me know that you care

In every way

Always there for me

Never letting me down

Only you can turn my frowns

Upside down

You lift my spirits

When I am my lowest

You take all the pain away

The greatest joy

Having you in my life

Just couldn't imagine you

not around

AFRAID

66

Longing to know your name

Imagining your hands

Waiting for the moment

Our lips finally meet

I love your style

Watching you

I float away

For just a little while

Handsome indeed

The naked eye

Can definitely see

But do you ever see me

In your world

I don't even exist

To have the courage

to open my mouth

To say hello or even hi

Nice weather

I think you're my perfect guy

I was terrified to utter

The slightest word

Again, I just keep my words inside

Behind my fears I hide

IS IT ME?

67

Is it me you want?

Is it me you need?

Is it me you can't live without?

Is it me you think about constantly?

Am I the one?

That brightens your day

When you look at me

Can you see our forever?

Is it me that you want?

To be your wife

To take that walk

Down the aisle

Is it me that you carry?

In your heart

Like, I carry you in mine

Am I the one that

you truly want

Is it me?

SWEET THOUGHTS OF YOU

68

Rain falling against my window

As I stare into space

Thoughts of you incomplete

I find myself thinking of you

All the time

As I twirl through my thoughts

I wonder how often do

you think of me

Not a moment

Not a day goes by

That you're not on my mind

As I think of you touching me

Amongst the most intimate feelings

A slight smile upon my face

Thoughts of you so deep

I can actually smell you

As if you were right here

This passion that I have for you

Arouses me in delicious ways

The delicate touch of your hand

The sweet taste of your lips

Let's me know

You are the man

CLOUDS OF US

69

As I look up deep into the clouds

It's as if I can see us

Your beautifully shaped lips

Coming to press against mine

Softly

We are happily engaged with us

These clouds tell a small story

As I continue to stare so high above

I see a storm forming

From a far

I hear thunder

Then a flash of lightning

Appeared in my sight

Then the hard cold rain

And we're gone

THE ANGER

70

So angry at times, I scare myself

The anger within has all control

I am helpless as a child

Looking for my mother

All I find is the anger

This anger fills my soul

I am so enraged

I smell my blood boil

It boils over and ruins it all

The anger has an impact

On my decisions

The anger, can't shake it

No matter how I try

The anger, my partner in crime

My life partner

As it seems

The anger

No matter, where I go

The anger, it's always near

Able to make me fear...myself

The anger, never fair but always here

AMNESIA

71

Who am I?

Where am I?

Can anyone help me?

Show me my way home

Where is home?

I don't know where to go

Which way to turn

Can anyone help me?

I cannot remember....anything

Are there people looking for me

Missing me

Am I a mother?

A sister

A niece

Who's child?

Who do I belong to?

Someone please help me

For, I am lost

So lost in this world

Amnesia, what is that?

A loss of memories and thoughts

Gone in a flash

CHANCE ENCOUNTER

72

Never thought about

Being in love

Wanting love

Needing love

Never in my life

Ever imagined this

Meeting you

Never believed in love

At first sight

Until, I met you

You, the best I ever knew

My strengths and weaknesses too

You know me to my heart

Takes you a part from any man

I have ever known

We have grown....together

To share this love

I hope forever

You are everything

DON'T LET ME FALL

73

Hold on to me

Please, never let me go

Without you

I am so vulnerable

With you

I feel like superwoman

There's nothing I cannot do

With my "S" on my chest

I can save the world

Hold on to me

Don't let me fall

It's a long way down

Falling out of your arms

Into an unknown world

I am so lost without you

You are everything and more

The many pleasures of you and I

I simply adore, so please

Hold on to me

Never let me go

Don't let me fall